For Jonah + Quinn Nov. 2017
from Great Aunt
Ursula. ☺ ♡

Printed in China
1 2 3 4 5 6 7 8 9 10
duopress
www.duopressbooks.com

Published simultaneously in Canada by Thomas Allen & Son Limited

Graphic Design: Erica Vermeulen

Special thanks to Bart B. Browne for his help on all the wacky art. You're an amazing illustrator and friend, Turtle Boy. —Jon

Library of Congress Cataloging-in-Publication Data

Names: Stollberg, Jon, illustrator.
Title: Totally epic, true & wacky soccer facts & stories by Puck / art by Jon Stollberg.
Description: First edition. | Baltimore, MD : duopress, [2017] | Audience: Ages: 9-12. | Audience: Grades: 4 to 6.
Identifiers: LCCN 2016032323| ISBN 9781938093814 (Trade Paper: alk. paper) | ISBN 9781938093821 (epub) | ISBN 9781938093838 (Kindle)
Subjects: LCSH: Soccer—Miscellanea—Juvenile literature. | Soccer—Pictorial works—Juvenile literature.
Classification: LCC GV943.25 .S78 2017 | DDC 796.334—dc23
LC record available at https://lccn.loc.gov/2016032323

TOTALLY Epic, True & WACKY SOCCER FACTS & STORIES

BY PUCK   ART BY JON STOLLBERG

duopress

Contents

Introduction

Soccer is played all over the world. With millions of fans and thousands of games played week after week, it's easy to hear epic stories of heroism and glory and tales about the great players and the amazing gooooooooooals!

But of course soccer also has a wild side. Some of the stories in this book are weird, a bit odd, and definitely crazy. Others are about amazing (and not so amazing) records and those passionate (and sometimes wild) fans in the stadiums.

So, trap the ball, start dribbling, and be ready for an epic run to the goal!

CHAPTER 1

You've Got to Be

Kidding Me!

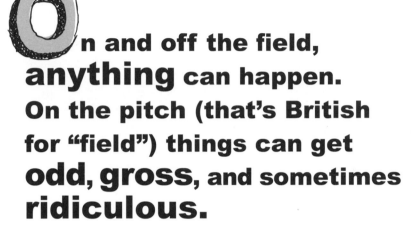

On and off the field, **anything** can happen. On the pitch (that's British for "field") things can get **odd, gross,** and sometimes **ridiculous.**

From floating soccer fields to megastars injuring themselves playing video games, these pages are your ticket to some of the wackiest moments of world soccer.

Chapter 1

You can buy a true-to-life sculpture of **Lionel Messi** for only $5 million. It is made of gold and was designed by a Japanese jeweler.

The shirt that Pelé wore during the final match of the 1970 World Cup, in which Brazil won its third World Cup trophy, was sold in 2002 for US $137,100.

Alfredo Di Stéfano, one of the best players in soccer history, built a monument for a soccer ball in his house. It's a ball made of bronze with a plaque that reads "Gracias, vieja." (Thanks, old woman.)

Old soccer stadiums didn't have many seats. Most fans watched the games standing on bleachers made of concrete.

What do **Cristiano Ronaldo**, **Neymar**, and **Carlos Tévez** have in common (beyond the fact that they are all great players)? They also share a birthday: **February 5**.

The record for the highest-altitude stadium belongs to the **Hernando Siles** Stadium in Bolivia. With an altitude of 2.23 miles (3.6 kilometers) above sea level, playing here leaves players gasping for breath.

The Float at Marina Bay is the biggest floating soccer stadium in the world. The pitch of the stadium floats on the waters of the Marina Reservoir in Singapore.

The Panyee Football Club on the island of Koh Panyee in Thailand needed a place to play their games. But finding a patch of grass on this tiny fishing island was impossible. Even the schools sit atop stilts here. So the kids decided to build a floating football field. Today, the Panyee Football Club is one of the best youth teams in Thailand!

Thousands of soccer fans gather every year to watch games played by elephants in Chitwan National Park in Nepal!

Perhaps the messiest form of soccer is swamp football. Six players per team play in a swamp and do their best to play the beautiful game. The Swamp Soccer World Cup is held in Scotland every year.

If you like both soccer and bike riding, then cycle ball is the sport for you. Also known as radball, this is a form of soccer where teams of two players ride bikes while controlling a ball with the wheels.

Golfoot is a mix of golf and soccer. The idea is to kick a ball into a hole, as in golf. Of course the holes are much bigger here.

Things seemed normal on the field when France was playing Kuwait during the 1982 World Cup in Spain—that is until a man wearing a robe, sandals, and a *kaffiyeh* (an Arab headdress) stormed onto the field to protest a goal. The man, a sheik and also president of the Kuwait Football Federation, was upset about what he thought was an illegal goal against his team. The referees were so confused that they agreed with him and changed their decision. France won the game 4 to 1, something no leader could have stopped.

A Japanese kid lost his soccer ball during the tsunami that hit Japan in 2011. The ball was found in Alaska two years later after traveling more than 3,000 miles (4,828 km) across the Pacific Ocean. The kid got his ball back.

Alaska

Japan

A 2001 study found that the jersey of a soccer player almost doubles in weight from the beginning of a game to the end. That's a lot of sweat!

13

Brazil and Italy were playing for a spot in the World Cup final in 1938. With only a few minutes left to play, the referee conceded a penalty for the Italians.

Giuseppe Meazza, an Italian striker, placed the ball in the penalty spot. A goal would put Italy in the final. With great determination, **Meazza** began his run, and just when he was about to kick the ball his shorts dropped. The spectators, the referee, and especially the Brazilian goalie didn't know what to make of this, but **Meazza** never hesitated, grabbing his falling shorts with one hand and kicking the ball with his powerful foot. He scored, and Italy played the final match a couple of days later. **Meazza** didn't score in the final match, but he kept his shorts up the entire game!

A goalie with team Medimurje in Croatia got a yellow card for getting a cat off of the field.

During a First Division game in Argentina, the referee sent off Paraguayan player **Celso Ayala**. The problem was that the ref had forgotten his red card in the locker room. **Ayala** refused to leave the pitch until somebody got the card to the ref. More than 10 minutes later, the ref finally showed **Ayala** the red card.

Carlos Fernando Navarro Montoya was a Colombian goalie with a bad temper. Once, after a big bout against players from Chilean team Colo Colo, he had to be restrained by the local police and a police dog named Ron. The canine bit the unruly goalie in his butt, and that was the end of the fight. Years after the game, Colo Colo fans still visit the tomb of the heroic Ron to remember the episode.

Goalies have a very low chance of stopping a penalty kick. This is interesting because in 1890 a player named **William McCrum** first proposed the penalty kick rule. **McCrum** played for an Irish team, as a goalie!

Goalies are on the field to stop goals, but some are actually very good at scoring goals! **José Luis Chilavert** (Paraguay) scored 67 goals in his career, including a hat trick in 1999. But the all-time goalie scoring record by far goes to Brazilian **Rogério Ceni,** who scored 130 goals in his career; 61 came as free kicks and 69 were from the penalty spot!

CHILAVERT

The semicircle at the top of the penalty area is known as the penalty arc. It is there to keep players from both teams away from the player taking the shot during a penalty kick. Although it is called the penalty arc, it is not part of the penalty area, so if a foul is committed inside the arc no penalty is given.

According to a study, players have a lower chance of scoring a penalty kick depending on the color of the goalie's shirt. The study found that players have the lowest success rate (54%) when the goalie is wearing red, followed by 69% when wearing yellow, 72% when wearing blue, and 75% when wearing green.

Italian defender **Alessandro Nesta** had surgery on his wrist after an injury. Nothing strange here, unless you consider that the famous defender was not hurt while playing soccer. It happened when he injured a tendon in his hand after playing PlayStation all night. **Nesta** didn't play soccer for a month after that.

You've Got to Be Kidding Me!

Argentinian striker **Martín Palermo** (a.k.a. el Loco) missed the 2002 World Cup after breaking his leg.

The injury came when he went crazy after scoring a goal and decided to celebrate by jumping into the crowd. It was fun, until the wall collapsed and crushed his leg.

Manchester United goalkeeper Alex Stephney liked to shout directions to his defenders. In 1975, he shouted so hard that he dislocated his jaw and had to leave the game.

Lionel Messi ended 2012 with an incredible goal average: 0.79 goals per game. **Sonia Bermúdez** from the FC Barcelona women's team had a better goal average: 1.16 goals per game!

17

Chapter 1

Being the son of a soccer legend doesn't mean you will be successful on the field. **Edinho** (the son of **Pelé**) wanted to be a goalie, but he played only 20 games in his career (and ended up in jail). **Stephan Beckenbauer** (the son of **Franz Beckenbauer**) became a soccer scout after failing to play for two German teams. And despite the fact that **Jordi Cruyff** (the son of **Johan Cruyff**) played for FC Barcelona and Manchester United, he ended his career without much success.

When two national teams face off on a soccer field, it is common for both of their national anthems to be played before kickoff. But with so many different teams, this can sometimes lead to problems. In World Cup 1930, the Yugoslavian players were outraged when the organizers played the Brazilian national anthem instead of their own. Since the game was in Uruguay, against the hosts, many people believe this was the Uruguayans' way to distract their rival. Suspiciously, the Yugoslavian flag was raised upside down, so perhaps the Yugoslavian players had good reason to be suspicious. Years later, during the Copa América Centenario 2016, it was the Uruguayan players who couldn't believe that the organizers played the Chilean national anthem instead of theirs!

Norway and Brazil played a decisive game during the 1998 World Cup in France. Before the game, Norwegian player Øivind Ekeland and his Brazilian fiancée, Rosangela de Souza, got married on the pitch. Norway beat Brazil 2–1 so it could be said that Ekeland won twice that day.

National anthem mix-ups also happen in friendly games. In 2015, El Salvador was playing against Argentina in Washington, D.C. The match had a weird start when the stadium played the national anthem of the Isle of Man! (This tiny island, located in the Irish Sea between Ireland and England, is a possession of the British crown, and yes, it has a national anthem.) The Salvadorian players were rightfully even more frustrated when they got an apology from the organizers for "playing the national anthem of Kazakhstan," which is an entirely different country!

"Good evening. The game you are about to see is the most stupid, appalling, disgusting, and disgraceful exhibition of football, possibly in the history of the game." This is how a British commentator introduced the airing of the game between Chile and Italy in World Cup 1962. The game, known as "the Battle of Santiago," is considered one of the most violent soccer games ever played. Police had to intervene at least four times to stop fighting between players on the field. Ouch!

The referee of the horrible match mentioned above was **Ken Aston.** Aston was so shocked by the violence he saw in the Battle of Santiago that years later he came up with the idea of using a yellow card to warn a player and a red card to eject the player from the field. Aston was inspired to create this system by a traffic light!

Ancient Greeks and Romans used an early version of soccer to train soldiers for battle.

When it comes to money there are no losing teams in the World Cup. FIFA gives $8 million to the teams eliminated in the first round. If a team comes in second, the $25 million FIFA gives it makes the sadness go away, but if a team wins the World Cup, it gets as much as $35 million. Oh, and the winning team gets a trophy, too.

Adidas is one of the biggest brands in soccer. In the final game of the 1990 World Cup between Argentina and Germany, everything on the field—the ball, the uniforms and shoes of all players, and the referee's and linemen's kits—was made by Adidas. A British reporter noted that only the referee's whistle was made by a different company.

21

José Andrade has been considered the first soccer superstar. The Uruguayan known as the Black Pearl won the Olympic gold in soccer in 1924 and 1928, as well as the 1930 World Cup for his country. **Andrade** liked to thrill soccer fans by traveling half of the field with the ball on his head.

Manchester United is known as the Red Devils, and they usually play in red uniforms. But in the 1996 season, somebody had the idea to change the color of the kits to gray. Fans hated it. Players hated it, and their legendary coach, Alex Ferguson, hated it even more. One time, during an away game that MU was losing 3–0, Ferguson ordered his players to change their shirts. Ferguson argued that his players couldn't see each other on the field in that color.

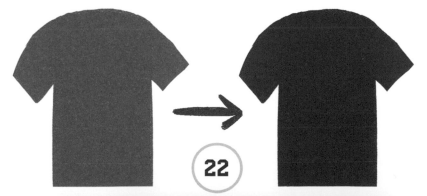

Before becoming a megastar with Manchester United, **David Beckham** was the team mascot. **Beckham** was 10 years old at the time. He later won six Premier League titles with the team.

Scottish goalie Chic Brodie tripped over a dog that ran onto the field during a match.

Brodie broke his knee in the incident and never played again.

23

Chapter 1

Bolivian star Marco Etcheverry debuted in the 1994 World Cup as a substitute in the 79th minute. He was shown a red card three minutes later. He never touched the ball!

Lionel Messi's debut with Argentina's national team was a huge event for the South American nation. Argentina was playing a friendly against Hungary. In the 65th minute, Lionel Messi came off the bench. Everybody in Argentina set their eyes on the substitute. Could this kid be their next soccer hero? The whole thing lasted 47 seconds. When Messi got the ball, he quickly dribbled a Hungarian defender. The defender grabbed Messi's shirt. Messi lifted his arm and tried to get away from him. The referee believed Messi elbowed the opponent. He called a foul and showed Messi a red card. Messi was out of the game less than a minute after coming onto the pitch.

Referees can show a red card for bad fouls and other violations, but some red cards have been shown in very strange situations. Chelsea star Eden Hazard was sent off after kicking a ball boy; British midfielder Mick O'Brien was shown a red card (twice!) for swinging on the crossbar (and breaking it!); Mexican coach Javier Aguirre saw a red card for tripping a player who was running along the sideline. And when a scantily clad invader decided to interrupt a game by running around the field, Dorchester player-manager Ashley Vickers thought that the police were too slow to get the intruder, so he decided to make a run and tackle the guy himself. He was given a red card by the ref for his actions.

Chapter 1

Turkish international **Arda Turan** was playing for Atlético de Madrid in a game against FC Barcelona. He was so frustrated with the game and the referees that he decided to throw his shoe at a linesman. Turan missed his target and, funny enough, he signed for FC Barcelona the next season.

There is a reason why superstar Diana Ross is a famous singer, not a footballer. During the opening ceremony of the 1994 USA World Cup, Ross performed one of her famous songs while running and dancing on the field. The grand finale was supposed to see Ross kick a ball, five yards out, and score a goal. But Ross missed the target, completely!

When a referee in Belorussia started to look odd on the field at the end of a game, some said that he looked drunk. Well, he was! A blood test showed that he had a little too much to drink before the game.

The field markings have to be 12 centimeters (4.72 inches) wide. These lines are usually white but can be orange or yellow. Interestingly enough, the goalposts also have to be 12 centimeters wide, but they must always be white.

Brazilian player **Garrincha** was knock-kneed (his knees were angled in and touched one another) and had a leg that was 2.3 inches (6 centimeters) longer than the other and a curved spine. Garrincha is considered one of the 10 best players in soccer history.

Players can get a yellow card for using a cell phone during a match. Also, they get a yellow card for smoking on the field, of course!

After scoring a goal for Nottingham Forest, **Billy Sharp** ran to the stands and celebrated by eating a fan's hot dog.

More countries belong to FIFA (Fédération Internationale de Football Association) than to the UN (United Nations).

At the end of the final game of the 1994 World Cup in Los Angeles, fans could buy grass from the field on which the game was played.

FOR SALE

Want your rival to fail? Bury some cats under their stadium. Seriously. This is what Argentinian club Independiente did after their local rivals, Racing of Avellaneda, won the Intercontinental Cup against Celtic of Scotland. As the story goes, while Racing fans were celebrating the victory, some jealous Independiente supporters sneaked into the stadium and buried seven dead black cats in different locations to bring bad luck to their archrivals. Did it work? Well, despite being one of the best clubs in Argentina, after the cats were buried, Racing did not win a single trophy for 35 years! And the next big win happened only after the team owners finally found the dead cats and took them out of the stadium! Weird? Yes. Effective? Perhaps. But please don't try this in your local travel-league games.

Two sets of famous twins that played for different professional teams are German-born Turkish footballers **Hamit** and **Halil Altıntop** and Argentinian duo **Guillermo** and **Gustavo Barros Schelotto**.

SCHELOTTO TWINS

HASSAN TWINS

The record for most games played by twins for their national team belongs to Hossam and Ibrahim Hassan for Egypt with a combined 309 caps. Frank and Ronald de Boar of the Netherlands come in second with a combined 179 games.

The **Hassan** twins scored 82 goals playing for Egypt while the **de Boar** twins scored 26 times combined. However, **Frank** and **Ronald de Boar** hold the record for eight World Cup matches played together!

Soccer is all about teamwork, so it helps when your twin brother plays for the same team. Famous twins Aleksei and Vasili Berezutski have played defense for CSKA Moskva and the Russian national team for many years. Goalkeeper Thomas Ravelli was famous for defending the Swedish national team net, and having his twin brother, Andreas, play center back probably helped him a lot. People used to joke that since Brazilian twins Rafael and Fabio Da Silva played the same position for Manchester United, they could have substituted for each other without anybody noticing.

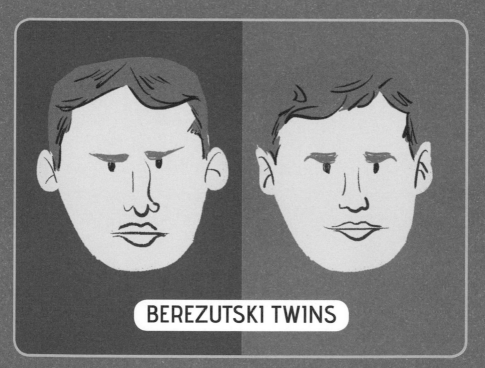

BEREZUTSKI TWINS

It's hard to be the coach. Coaches in soccer, as in other sports, lose their jobs frequently, usually when the team is not playing well or getting the right results. In the 2007–2008 season, for example, 63 coaches lost their jobs in the five largest European leagues!

In that 2007–2008 season, the Italian Serie A sacked 26 coaches, and 14 lost their jobs in La Liga (Spain), 12 in the Premier League (England), 6 in the Bundesliga (Germany), and 5 in La Ligue (France).

The coach with the shortest job has to be Leroy Rosenior, who was hired by English team Torquay United in 2007, only to lose his job 10 minutes later when the team announced that it had been sold and the new owners wanted to work with another coach!

Followers of Hartlepool United in England attended the last game of the 2012 season dressed like Smurfs. A year later they dressed as penguins.

In 2011, the Turkish Football Federation banned **Fenerbahçe** adult and teenage male supporters from their stadium for five games due to their bad behavior during a match. During that time only female and children supporters cheered for the famous Turkish team.

Italian player Sebastián Giovinco played with number 12 on his jersey for Italian team Juventus. On 12/12/2012, he scored a goal in the 12th minute of the second half.

During a game between Liverpool and Sunderland in the English Premier League, a young Liverpool fan threw a balloon onto the field. When a Sunderland player tried to shoot a goal, the ball hit the balloon, changed direction, and ended in the net. Not cool, unless, of course, you are a Sunderland fan.

Twenty trains were used to light up the first evening soccer game played in Brazil in 1923.

SEELER   PÉLE

Two players have scored at least one goal in four different World Cups: **Pelé** (Brazil) and **Uwe Seeler** (West Germany).

Argentinian striker Gabriel Batistuta scored hat tricks in two consecutive World Cups: in the United States in 1994 and in France in 1998. What makes this odd is that both feats happened the same day: June 21.

The Indian soccer federation refused to participate in the 1950 World Cup in Brazil after FIFA declined their request for Indian players to play without shoes. Some Indian players were actually used to playing barefoot and had played like this in the Olympic Games. So the mandatory boots came as a surprise to them.

If you love Christmas, you may want to become a fan of a team in Finland. Its name: FC Santa Claus. As expected the team's uniform is red!

Usain Bolt, Olympic gold medalist in the 100 and 200 meter sprints, loves soccer. The sprinter signed with British powerhouse Manchester United for a charity game.

Some children in Indonesia play a dangerous form of soccer. Instead of using a regular ball, they fill a coconut with fuel and light it on fire. If that's not freaky enough, these guys play without shoes. Ouch!

Goals by **heading** the ball are normally scored at close range. But check this out: **Jone Samuelsen**, a Norwegian midfielder, scored a goal with his head from behind the midfield line in 2011. The ball traveled 187 feet (57 meters) before reaching the net! The question is, where was the goalie?

Researchers have found that 37% of children who play soccer get better grades than their peers.

April 14 is International Goalkeeper Day. Don't score a goal against one that day.

During a game between teams from Iran and Saudi Arabia in 2012, an Iranian player picked up a strange object from the field and threw it out of the pitch. The object was a hand grenade, and it exploded the moment it hit the ground!

Chapter 1

The award for the biggest dive or fake in soccer goes to **Allan Simonsen** of the Danish national team who faked his own death during a World Cup qualifier match in 1977. As it turns out, a film director wanted to do a scene for a movie in which a player was shot in the back during a major game. The problem was that the director didn't have the money to create the elaborate scene, so he gave some money to **Simonsen** to fake the scene during a real game! During the match, **Simonsen**'s team had a corner kick. He made a run to the penalty box, and as the cross came in he threw himself to the ground as if he had been shot in he back! His team, by the way, lost the game and didn't make it to the World Cup.

But the award for most outrageous fake of all time has to go to Chilean goalkeeper Roberto Antonio Rojas, who tried to fool the referee by hurting himself, for real. This happened in a game against Brazil. Chile needed a good result to qualify for the World Cup, and since Brazil was playing, and winning, at home **Rojas** decided to pretend that an object was thrown at him from the stands. When the referee came to check on him, **Rojas**'s face was bleeding. Chilean players were outraged and abandoned the field. The idea was for the game to be canceled and they would be awarded a win. However, a photograph showed that nothing had hit **Rojas** and that he had concealed a small blade in his gloves. You can see where this is going. **Rojas** had cut his own face! Officials gave the win to Brazil, and **Rojas** was banned from football for life.

Diego Armando Maradona of Argentina scored two of the most famous goals in the history of soccer in the same game, one for being controversial and the other for its absolute beauty. Known as "the Hand of God goal" and "the Goal of the Century," the two goals were scored four minutes apart in a quarterfinal World Cup match between Argentina and England in 1986.

Maradona's "Hand of God goal" was the result of a play were **Maradona** apparently headed the ball into the net. However, the Argentinian superstar had used his hand, right above his head, to push the ball into the goal. When asked about the incident, **Maradona** said that the goal was scored "a little with his head and a little with the hand of God."

Maradona's "Goal of the Century" started when he took the ball inside his own half and began a 60-yard (55-m) run toward the English goal. **Maradona** skillfully dribbled four players, one of them twice, and then tricked the goalkeeper before putting the ball into the net. Argentina won the match 2–0 and went on to become world champions a few days later.

Zinedine Zidane, considered one of the best 10 players in history and winner of the FIFA World Player of the Year three times, is known for his suave style and amazing technique. Unfortunately, the French superstar is also well known for head-butting an Italian defender in the chest after a heated discussion during the 2006 World Cup final match. Zidane was sent off, and France lost the game in penalty kicks.

• • • • • • • • • • • • • • • • • • • •

Zidane's head-butt to **Marco Materazzi** became so famous that it has been spoofed in the TV show *Family Guy* when an animated **Zidane** head-butts an old lady, and has been represented in a bronze sculpture by an Algerian artist (**Zidane** is of Algerian descent) that was unveiled in 2012.

43

Chapter 1

$\mathcal{S}$ome toddlers bite when they lose control, and so does **Luis Suárez**, one of the best strikers on the planet. There have been at least three incidents where the Uruguayan forward has bitten an opposing player for no good reason. And really, there is never a good reason to bite another human being. The most "famous" bite happened during the 2014 World Cup match between Uruguay and Italy, when **Suárez** clashed with Italian defender **Giorgio Chiellini** while waiting for a cross. Both players fell to the ground, and **Chiellini** quickly showed the referee some nasty teeth marks on his shoulder. **Suárez** stayed on the ground holding his front teeth in pain. **Suárez** did not get a red card, but he was banned for nine international matches and from participating in any soccer activity for four months. That's a big time-out!

The club of dirty players is not just for boys. **Elizabeth Lambert**, a footballer from the University of New Mexico (USA), was suspended from the team after committing a series of violent fouls. Kicking, pushing, and tackling players with unnecessary force is—unfortunately—common among some soccer players, and **Lambert** did plenty of that, but when she was caught on video pulling the hair of an opponent and dragging her to the ground that was the end of her college soccer career.

LAMBERT SUSPENDED

Don't Drop the Trophy (Seriously!)

Winning a **trophy** is hard, and it seems that some winning **teams** are not really careful with their **reward.** Here is look at some **notorious** cup plunges, steals, and disappearances.

1968

The World Cup trophy, known as the Jules Rimet Trophy, is stolen in England. A week later it is found in a ditch by a dog named Pickles.

1983

The Jules Rimet Trophy disappears (again!) in Brazil. It is never found!

2002

During FC Schalke's celebratory parade, the German FA Cup slips from the hands of one team staff member. It takes five months of work by an expert goldsmith to repair the trophy.

2011

In Spain, Real Madrid needed 18 years to win the Copa del Rey once again, but it took only a few seconds for defender **Sergio Ramos** to drop the trophy from the bus used for the celebratory parade. The trophy was crushed under the bus's wheels.

2011

Ajax goalkeeper **Maarten Stekelenburg's** hands stopped many goals during a tournament, but when his team was riding through Amsterdam to show the Eredevisie trophy to their fans, he couldn't hold the trophy and dropped it onto the road.

2012

Ajax wins the Dutch League again, and this time it is defender **Jan Vertonghen** who drops the Eredevisie trophy. It lands on his foot, and **Vertonghen** continues with the parade with a bloody sock.

CHAPTER 2
There's a First Time for
Everything

We call **soccer** the **beautiful** game, but before it became the sport we know today it was a pretty **messy** event. With time, rules were written, a proper **field** was established, and **punching** and **kicking** other players was not cool anymore. One day, a player tried a crazy trick and invented a bicycle kick; another wanted to look different and wore colored cleats. Everything you love about soccer happened once for the first time, and here you can enjoy some of these **legendary** firsts!

Soccer players couldn't wear shorts until 1901. Before that they wore knickers, or loose-fitting pants that ended at the knees.

Shin guards were invented in 1874 but didn't become mandatory for all players on the field until 1990.

Soccer cleats can be made from different plastics, fabrics, and leather. The most popular leather, known for its strong and flexible characteristics, comes from kangaroos.

Goalies didn't start wearing special gloves until the 1970s. German keeper **Sepp Maier** was the first to wear terry cloth–padded gloves with rubber pieces. Before **Maier**, goalies wore gloves made of rough wood or leather.

Today it's common to see goalies playing the ball with their feet, and some of them do it really well. But it wasn't until the 1970s that they were allowed to take this risk. Dutch coach **Rinus Michels**, the creator of so-called Total Football, was the first to ask goalies to play as extra defenders and to play 20 yards (18.2 m) from their goal. It was a risky move, but much of the success of teams like Ajax, Barcelona, and Bayern Munich is based on this tactic.

Before 1870, teams didn't have a dedicated goalkeeper. It wasn't until 1909 that goalkeepers where required to wear a different colored uniform.

Numbers on the back of jerseys in a World Cup were used for the first time during the 1950 tournament played in Brazil.

n 1863 it was decided to use two goalpost 8 yards (7.32 m) apart to mark the goal. The distance between the two posts hasn't changed in more than 150 years.

. . . .

The original goalposts didn't have a crossbar, which allowed players to score a goal even if the ball crossed the line really high. A goal back then would have looked a little bit like a field goal in American football.

. . . .

Having no crossbars wasn't fair to the goalies. How could a goalie stop a ball 30 feet (10 m) in the air? So, in 1872 somebody thought that it would be a good idea to tie a long piece of tape from one goalpost to the other.

he tape idea didn't last, and real crossbars were introduced in soccer in 1882.

In 1889, British inventor John Alexander Brodie invented the goal net. No more chasing after a ball!

Today's goalposts are round, but before 1961 they were square. Not surprisingly, injuries from crashing into or hitting the posts have been reduced since then.

uring a European Cup semifinal between Real Madrid and Borussia Dortmund, fans start shaking the fence that divides the stadium and the pitch until it collapsed. With the fence came the goalposts, and the game had to be delayed 75 minutes until a truck was able to bring a new goalpost from a nearby training ground.

The first time ball boys and ball girls were used to return the balls to the field was during the World Cup in England in 1966. The question is who returned the balls before that?

Before the 1970s, all players wore either black or brown soccer boots. Alan Ball of British club Everton was the first player to wear a different color when he played in white boots.

Colored cleats didn't become a trend until 1973 when Swedish player Conny Torstensson wore red shoes when scoring two goals in a European Cup game against Bayern Munich.

Today, almost no professional player wears brown or black shoes, and colors can range from bright green and yellow to pink and multicolor.

Charles Goodyear is credited with the invention of vulcanized rubber, which is used in car tires and many other objects, like the soccer ball. His invention allowed for more spherical (fancy word for "round") balls. The first soccer ball based on his invention was used for a soccer game in Boston in 1863.

Goodyear's invention was awesome, but soccer balls needed laces to tie them together. That was not good news when a player needed to do a header. The laces made heading the ball so painful that most players simply avoiding doing it altogether. Ouch!

In the 1930s, three Argentines named **Tossolini**, **Valbonesi**, and **Polo** created a chamber with a valve that allowed a ball to be inflated by injecting air into it. Even better, the ball didn't need laces anymore so players began to head the ball more often, creating new strategies and skills.

56

occer balls were made of leather until the 1950s. Leather balls were much heavier than the balls used today. And on rainy days, leather balls almost doubled in weight.

Early soccer balls were made out of skulls or inflated pig bladders. Poor goalies!

The first ball made "official" for a World Cup was the Telstar in Mexico in 1970. The ball had 32 black and white panels to make it easier to see on black and white televisions. That made sense, since the 1970 World Cup was the first to be broadcast live on television.

After the first official Telstar ball, other special balls have been designed for the World Cup: Telstar Durlast for Germany 1974, Tango Durlast for Argentina 1978, Tango España for Spain 1982, Azteca for Mexico 1986, Etrusco in Italy 1990, Questra for USA 1994, Triciolore in France 1998, and Fevernova for Korea-Japan in 2002. All these balls had 32 panels.

The first ball specifically designed for the Women's World Cup was the Icon for the tournament played in the United States in 1999.

The Teamgeist was the first ball designed for a World Cup that wasn't built by stitching 32 panels. The use of round and other shaped panels revolutionized the soccer ball by reducing imperfections. It was first used in the World Cup in Germany in 2006.

Since, the Teamgeist soccer balls have continue to evolve: The Jabulani used in World Cup South Africa 2010 used special 3-D panels (*Jabulani* means "to celebrate"). The Brazuca used in World Cup Brazil 2014 was built with six identical panels and was tested by 600 of the world's top players in 10 countries. The name "Brazuca" was selected in a public vote of one million Brazilian fans. The name describes the Brazilian way of life.

The first World Cup tournament that used a mascot was in England 1966. The mascot's name was **Willie**, a lion with a jersey with the British flag. Since then every World Cup had used a mascot to promote the tournament.

At least one of the following four national teams has played in each World Cup final: Brazil, Germany, Italy, and Argentina.

ARGENTINA   ITALY   BRAZIL   GERMANY

The first World Cup game shown live on TV was during the World Cup in Switzerland in 1954. Four million people watched the Yugoslavian national team beat France 1–0. Sixty years later, 696 million people watched the final game of the World Cup Brazil 2014.

There's a First Time for Everything

The first activity that resembles today's soccer was recorded in China in the third century BCE. The game was named Tsu Chu and consisted of kicking a ball toward a small net.

· ·

Students in England first used the word "soccer" in the 19th century.

The first international match was played between Scotland and England in 1872. As of this writing, these countries have played against each other 112 times. England has won 77 times, Scotland has won 24 times, and 41 games have ended in a draw.

VS.

Today, a team can make three substitutions. Until 1970, teams could only substitute the goalies, and only if they were hurt.

Today, soccer teams switch sides at halftime. This hasn't always been the rule. Before 1872, the teams switched sides after each goal.

The first official women's soccer game was played in Glasgow, Scotland, in 1892.

Many experts agree that the first bicycle kick happened when Ramón Unzaga, a Chilean defender, performed the acrobatic move around 1914. This spectacular kick continues to be called "Chilena" in Spanish-speaking countries, and it is also known as an overhead kick or a scissor kick.

In 1981, A.C. Milan became the first team to print the name of its players on the back of the jerseys.

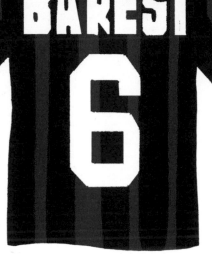

• • • • • • • • • • • • •

The so-called **Mexican Wave**, where continuous groups of fans stand, yell, raise their arms, and sit right after, became popular worldwide during the World Cup in Mexico in 1986. But the Wave was first performed in a baseball stadium in Oakland, California, in the 1970s and became popular during college football games in Seattle, Washington, in the 1980s. So, let's just call it the **Crazy Wave**.

Before using a whistle, referees used a handkerchief to announce their calls. It wasn't until 1878 that the first whistle was utilized.

Referees dressed in black when soccer first started. It wasn't until World Cup 1994 that referees had the option to wear jerseys of one of three colors: burgundy, yellow, or white.

The color of the referee's jersey has to contrast with the colors of the uniforms of the two teams playing the game. This is to avoid confusion since no player wants to pass the ball to the referee!

Yellow and red cards were introduced during the 1970 World Cup in Mexico. The yellow card is shown as a warning, and the red is shown to send a player off of the field.

Before somebody came up with the great idea of using a referee, the captains of both teams would debate their disagreements.

65

CHAPTER **3**

Records

Winning may be everything, but **how** you win (or lose) may be just as important. Scoring five goals in one game is really hard, but scoring five goals in less than nine minutes becomes a **record**. A winning streak is great; a losing one, not so much. Soccer is full of **record-breaking** moments. Some are epic, others are shameful, but once the **feat** has been recorded it will be there forever. That is until somebody else achieves another incredible act or does something even **sillier**.

The San Marino national team spent 18 years without winning a single game, from 1986 to 2004. A 1–0 friendly win against the Liechtenstein national team is their only win in history!

It's hard to score five goals in a professional game, but Robert Lewandowski not only scored five times, he did it in less than nine minutes. This incredible feat by the Bayern Munich striker recorded in September 2015 gets even better. Lewandowski came off the bench and scored his first three goals in less than four minutes!

Real Madrid didn't lose a single game playing in their stadium from 1957 to 1965. Madrid was unbeaten at home for 22 games!

The Azteca Stadium in Mexico City has witnessed two of the best soccer players in the world lift the World Cup trophy: Pelé (1970) and Diego Armando Maradona (1986).

PELÉ   MARADONA

M

ário Zagallo (Brazil) and **Franz Beckenbauer** (Germany) share an incredible record. They both won World Cups as players and as coaches. As a player, **Zagallo** won in 1958 and 1962 and lifted the cup as coach in 1970. **Beckenbauer** won as a player in 1974 and as team boss in 1990.

• •

Seven players have won the Champions League as players and coaches: **Miguel Muñoz**, **Pep Guardiola**, and **Luis Enrique** (Spain); **Giovanni Trapattoni** and **Carlo Ancelotti** (Italy); and **Frank Rijkaard** and **Johan Cruyff** (Netherlands).

ZAGALLO

ANCELOTTI   CRUYFF   ENRIQUE   MUÑOZ

TRAPATTONI   BECKENBAUER   GUARDIOLA   RIJKAARD

Like father like son: **Cesare Maldini** and his son **Paolo** won six Champions League titles with Italian team A.C. Milan. **Cesare** won the tournament in 1963, while **Paolo** won it five times (1988, 1990, 1994, 2003, and 2007).

The son of **Paolo Maldini** (and grandson of **Cesare**) is an up-and-coming star. **Christian Maldini** is only 20 years old, but soccer fans are already excited to see this third-generation **Maldini** on a famous team.

Christian Maldini is not the only son of a legend with chances to play professionally in the next few years. Can you imagine a team with **Christian Maldini**, **Brooklyn Beckham** (son of **David Beckham**), **Enzo Zidane** (son of **Zinedine Zidane**), and **Romarinho** (son of **Romario**)?

Edson Arantes do Nascimento, better known as Pelé, is the player with the most goals scored in soccer. The Brazilian megastar found the net 1,279 times from 1956 to 1977. His Milésimo goal (1,000th) was a penalty while playing for his club Santos at the Maracanã Stadium in Rio de Janeiro.

As impressive as it is, Pelé's record includes goals scored in friendly and other non-official matches. The record for most goals scored in official games belongs to Josef Bican, a Czech-Austrian striker who found the net 805 times while playing for seven different clubs and two national teams.

Only one shot of every ten is a goal. So, keep shooting.

Abby Wambach (USA) leads the list of women top scorers in international games with 184 goals. **Wambach** is followed by **Christine Sinclair** (Canada, 161 goals); **Mia Hamm** (USA, 158 goals); **Kristine Lilly** (USA, 130), and **Birgit Prinz** (Germany, 128 goals).

The record for most goals scored in a single international game belongs to **Jean Kaltack** from the small island nation of Vanuatu. **Kaltack** scored 16 goals in a game against Micronesia during the 2015 Pacific Games. The final score was 46–0 for **Kaltack**'s team!

Running and endurance are very important in soccer. But it hasn't always been like this. In 1958, when **Pelé** played his first World Cup, a player would run an average of 2.4 miles (4 km) in one game. Today, players can easily run 7 miles (11.2 km) in a game.

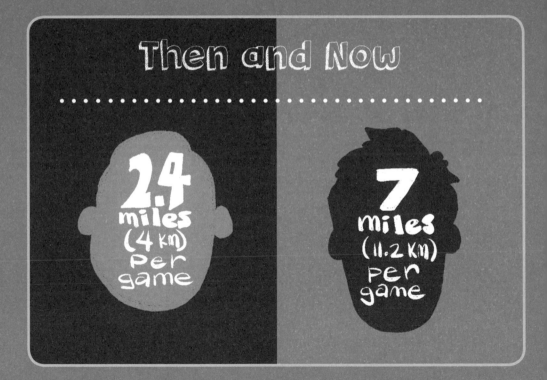

Then and Now

2.4 miles (4 km) per game

7 miles (11.2 km) per game

Average by Position

Midfielders	Forwards	Defenders	Goalies
7.5 miles	7 miles	6.21 miles	2.5 miles

Central midfielder **Marcelo Diaz** of Chile ran the greatest distance of any player in the first two games of the 2014 World Cup in Brazil. **Diaz** totaled 15.72 miles (25.2 km) in two matches. That's a lot of running!

Midfielders cover the most distance of the players on the field per match: 7.5 miles (12 km) on average. Forwards cover an average of 7 miles (11.25 km), and defenders cover 6.21 miles (10 km) per game. Goalies run an average of 2.5 miles (4 km) in a match.

A soccer referee can cover up to 8 miles (13 km) in a game. So, it often turns out that they run more than the players!

Two Argentinian teams needed 44 penalties in a penalty shoot-out to decide a winner in 1989. But that is not the record for the longest professional penalty shoot-out of all time. This record belongs to two teams playing for the Namibian Cup Final in 2005. KK Palace and Civics needed 48 penalty kicks to decide the winner. KK Palace prevailed, and the final score was 17–16.

Three players have each played in five World Cups. Two of them are goalies: **Antonio Carbajal** played for Mexico in 1950, 1954, 1958, 1962, and 1966; **Gianluigi Buffon** has played for Italy in 1998, 2002, 2006, 2010, and 2014. (And he could actually play in another World Cup!) The only outfield player in this group is **Lothar Matthäus,** who played for Germany in 1982, 1986, 1990, 1994, and 1998.

It's good to play for Germany since all of the players with the most games played in World Cup history are German: **Miroslav Klose** (29 matches), **Philipp Lahm** (27), **Bastian Schweinsteiger** (26), **Per Mertesacker** (25), and **Lothar Matthäus** (25).

MATTHÄUS 25   KLOSE 29   LAHM 27   SCHWEINSTEIGER 26   MERTESACKER 25

Russian player Oleg Salenko is the player with the most goals in one World Cup match; he scored five goals in Russia's 6–1 defeat over Cameroon in the World Cup USA 1994.

SALENKO

American player Michelle Akers is the player with most goals in one Women's World Cup match. Akers scored five goals when the USA defeated Chinese Taipei 7–0 in the 1991 Women's World Cup played in China.

AKERS

Tim Howard **of the United States has the record of most shots saved in one World Cup match. Howard saved his goal 15 times in a game against Belgium in 2014. Unfortunately, sometimes a great goalie can't win a game, and USA lost the match.**

The game between the United States and Portugal in the 2002 World Cup has a strange record. This is the only game in World Cup history in which a player from each team scored in his own goal: **Jeff Agoos** for USA and **Jorge Costa** for Portugal. USA won the match 3–2, though.

AGOOS   COSTA

On the other hand, Dutch player **Ernie Brandts** scored two goals in a game against Italy in the World Cup 1978. Brandts scored in his own net in the 18th minute and on the Italian goal in the 50th minute. In the end, the Netherlands won 2 goals to 1.

Stan Van Den Buijs scored three own goals during a game in the Belgian league. His team, Germinal Ekeren, lost 3–2.

Madagascan team Stade Olympique protested a questionable penalty against their team by scoring their own goals from the kickoff spot. They did it over and over, and the final score was Stade Olympique 0, AS Adema 149!

OOPS!

Serbian coach **Bora Milutinović** has never coached his home country, but he has coached the most national teams in World Cups. **Milutinović** has coached five different countries: Mexico (1986), Costa Rica (1990), United States (1994), Nigeria (1998), and China (2002).

MONDRAGÓN

WHITESIDE

The oldest player to participate in a World Cup game is **Faryd Mondragón** of Colombia. The youngest is **Norman Whiteside** of Northern Ireland. **Mondragón** was 43 years and 1 day old; **Whiteside** was 17 years, 1 month, and 10 days old. That's a 26-year difference!

ZIDANE **MÁRQUEZ** **CAFU**

Zinedine **Zidane** of France, **Rafaél Márquez** of Mexico, and **Cafu** of Brazil share the highest number of penalty cards in World Cup history: **Zidane** is the "winner" of this category with four yellow and two red cards. **Márquez** had five yellow cards and one red. The good boy here is **Cafu**, who got six yellow cards but was never shown a red card.

· ·

José Batista of Uruguay holds the shameful record of seeing the fastest red card in a World Cup match. Batista was sent off only 56 seconds after the beginning of the game.

Claudio Caniggia of Argentina didn't even need the 56 seconds to see the red card. After excessive complaining and berating the official, he was sent off from the bench in a match against Sweden in the World Cup 2002.

The match with the most goals in World Cup history was between Austria and Switzerland in 1954. The score was 7–5. That's 12 goals in a game, but it was a close match. The most uneven match saw "only" 11 goals when Hungary defeated El Salvador 10 goals to 1 in 1982.

HUNGARY **10**   EL SALVADOR **1**

FINAL

Brazil is the team with the most matches won in World Cup history with 70. Germany is a close second with 66, followed by Italy with 45.

70   **66**   **45**

Brazil also holds the record for the largest defeat ever suffered by a host team when Germany beat them 7–1 during the World Cup 2014 in Brazil.

Five countries have hosted the World Cup twice: Mexico, Italy, Germany, France, and Brazil. Only Mexico hasn't won the World Cup.

Six countries have won the World Cup while hosting the tournament: Uruguay (1930), Italy (1934), England (1966), Germany (1974), Argentina (1978), and France (1998).

South Africa (2010) is the only country that was eliminated in the first round while hosting the World Cup.

Spain (1982) and the United States (1994) were eliminated in the second round in the World Cups they hosted.

In women's soccer history, the teams with the most victories are USA with 33 wins followed by Germany with 26 wins.

The USA national women's team has won more World Cups than any other country. The USA won the cup three times, in 1991, 1999, and 2015. The Germans are in second with two World Cup trophies (2003, 2007). Only two other teams have won the Women's World Cup: Norway (1995) and Japan (2011).

Japan, Brazil, Germany, Nigeria, Norway, and USA have participated in more Women's World Cups than any other countries. Each of these six teams has played in seven World Cups.

Lionel Messi (Argentina) is the only player that has won the Ballon d'Or (Golden Ball) for best player in the world five times, all while playing for FC Barcelona.

Messi scored 50 goals in the 2011–12 season playing for FC Barcelona.

Cristiano Ronaldo (Portugal) is the only player who has won the European Golden Shoe, the award given to Europe's leading scorer, while playing in two different leagues. **Ronaldo** first won with 31 goals in the Premier League (England) playing with Manchester United. Three years later he won the award for scoring 40 goals in La Liga (Spain), playing for Real Madrid.

Three North American female players have won the FIFA World Player of the Year; **Mia Hamm** won it twice, while **Abby Wambach** and **Carli Lloyd** have each won it once.

In 2013, Mia Hamm became the first woman to be inducted into the Football Hall of Fame.

Abby Wambach has scored more international goals than any other player in women's soccer. Wambach found the net 184 times! Second place belongs to **Christine Sinclair** of Canada (161 goals), and third place goes to **Mia Hamm**, who scored 158 international goals in 275 games with Team USA.

In women's soccer, Marta (Brazil) has won the FIFA World Player of the Year five times, followed by Birgit Prinz (Germany), who has won it two times.

THE WORLD'S RICHEST TEAMS ARE ALL IN EUROPEAN LEAGUES:

1. Real Madrid (La Liga, Spain)
2. FC Barcelona (La Liga, Spain)
3. Manchester United (Premier League, England)
4. Manchester City (Premier League, England)
5. FC Bayern Munich (Bundesliga, Germany)

IN THE AMERICAS, THE FIVE RICHEST TEAMS ARE IN THREE COUNTRIES:

1. S.C. Corinthians (Série A, Brazil)
2. Grêmio FBPA (Série A, Brazil)
3. Palmeiras (Série A, Brazil)
4. C.D. Guadalajara (Liga MX, Mexico)
5. New York Red Bulls (MLS, USA)

- The world's most followed teams on Facebook are: FC Barcelona, Real Madrid CF, Manchester United FC, Chelsea FC, FC Bayern Munich
- Most followed players are: **Cristiano Ronaldo**, **Lionel Messi**, **Neymar**, **David Beckham**, **Ronaldinho**

CHAPTER **4**

What's in a
Name?

World **soccer** is full of **colorful** names and some crazy **nicknames**. No player likes to be called the **Butcher** or the **Little Donkey**, but once a nickname sticks, the soccer **universe** will repeat it **forever**. This is not always bad. Everybody knows Edson Arantes do **Nascimento** as Pelé, and his nickname is the **King**. That sounds great, but nicknames are not always that, ahem, **uplifting**.

Cristiano Ronaldo, whose full name is **Cristiano Ronaldo dos Santos Aveiro**, got his middle name, **Ronaldo**, because his parents admired **Ronald Reagan**, the United States president.

The Colombian striker **Carlos Darwin Quintero** was named after British scientist **Charles Darwin** ("Carlos" is "Charles" in Spanish). His nickname is the **Scientist of the Goal**!

Some famous players have gotten their nicknames based on video games or superheroes. Mario Basler (Germany) was known as Super Mario, and Argentinian Gabriel Batistuta was nicknamed Batigol ("**Batman**" plus "**goal**"). Chilean forward Iván Zamorano's looks resembled a baby from the *Flintstones* cartoon so he spent a successful career with the label of Bam Bam Zamorano.

Many Brazilian players like to be known only by their first name or their nickname. Not many people know the name **Ricardo Izecson dos Santos Leite**, but everybody knows this superstar's nickname: **Kaká**.

It's not clear how **Edson Arantes do Nascimento** came to be called **Pelé**, but he was such a great player that he earned a royal nickname: O Rei (the King). Of course, many players have aspired to be as good as the King, and some of their nicknames are based on **Pelé**'s reputation: **Tostão** and **Zico**, two other fantastic Brazilian players, were nicknamed **Pelé Blanco** (White Pelé).

Diego Armando Maradona is known as **Pelusa** (Scruffy), and some players around the world are named after the great Argentinian, such as **Saeed Al-Owairan** (Saudi Arabia), known as the **Maradona of the Desert**, and **Gheorghe Hagi** (Romania), who besides being called the **Commander** was known as the **Maradona of the Carpathians** (the Carpathian Mountains are a mountain range in Romania).

. . . .

Other interesting nicknames have been given to **Marcelo Gallardo** (Argentina), who was known as El Muñeco (the Doll); **Claudio Pizarro** (Peru) aka **Pizza**; **Eric Wynalda** (USA), called **Waldo** or the **Cannon**; **Zinedine Zidane** (France) known as **Zizou**; and **Roberto Baggio** (Italy), whose good looks and famous hairstyle earned him the nickname of **Il Divin Codino** (the Divine Ponytail).

. . . .

Juan Ramón Verón (Argentina) was known as **La Bruja** (the Witch), so when his son **Juan Sebastián** became a soccer player, he was nicknamed **La Brujita** (the Little Witch).

Nicknames after animals are common in all sports. In soccer, some reflect the power of the player: **Eusébio** (Portugal) was known as the **Black Panther, Faustino Asprilla** (Colombia) was the **Black Gazelle**, and **Johan Neeskens** (Netherlands) was nicknamed the **Bull**. Other players' nicknames follow the animal trend, but they don't sound quite as powerful, such as **Ariel Ortega** (Argentina) aka the **Little Donkey** or **Miguel Pardeza** (Spain), who was known as the **Little Rat**.

The name of Swedish superstar **Zlatan Ibrahimovi** reflects his big personality: "**Zlatan**" means "made of gold."

Javier Hernández (Mexico) is known as **Chicharito** (Little Pea). The nickname comes from his father, also a famous soccer player, who had green eyes. Since peas are green he was called **Chicharo** (Pea).

Nicknames sometimes come from a player's reputation. Spanish defender **Andoni Goikoetxea**, known as the **Butcher of Bilbao**, was feared by his rivals because of his rough style. German striker **Gerd Müller** scored 14 goals in the two World Cups he played. His explosive style earned him the nickname of the **Bomber**. And Dutch midfielder **Willy Van der Kerkhof** was so good at recovering the ball that he was known as the **Vacuum Cleaner**.

. . . .

Lionel Messi is known for his small stature, which is fine since "Lionel" means "**small lion**."

· ·

The first name of legendary Spanish goalie **Iker Casillas** means "**bearer of good news**." His parents were right to give him this name since his skills helped Spain win their first World Cup title in 2010.

Brazilians use more than 30 synonyms for **"soccer ball."** Some of these are **woman, baby, balloon, capricious one, demon, doll, and chestnut.**

HOW DO YOU SAY "SOCCER" IN DIFFERENT LANGUAGES?
British English: football; **Italian**: calcio; **Portuguese**: futebol; **Japanese**: futtoboru; **Spanish**: fútbol; **Chinese**: 足球 (zúqiú); **Zulu**: ibjoa; **Vietnamese**: bōng dā; **Russian**: футбольный (futbol'nyy); **French**: football.

NATIONAL TEAM NICKNAMES

Every national soccer team has a nickname. Some are obvious, some are fun, and some are a little weird. Here is a list of just a few.

Algeria, "Les Fennecs." The fennec is the national animal of Algeria. This small nocturnal fox native to North Africa inspires the fast-paced game of the Algerian players.

Argentina, "La Albiceleste." *Albiceleste* means "white and blue sky," and you can see those two colors on Argentina's famous striped uniforms.

Australia, "the Socceroos." This fun nickname combines the words "soccer" and "kangaroos."

Belgium, "Red Devils." This spirited name was first used after a journalist described three "devilish" wins in 1906 by the Belgian squad.

Bosnia and Herzegovina, "Zmajevi."
Bosnia and Herzegovina players were described as *zmajevi*, or "dragons," by a local commentator in 2010. Players and fans liked it, and since then the team has been known by this cool nickname.

Brazil, "La Seleção." Simply put *Seleção* means "the Selection" in Portuguese. Since a national team is a selection of a country's best players, the name makes perfect sense. The Brazilian team is also known as "La Canarinha" (Little Canary) because of their yellow shirts; the "Verde-Amarela" (the Green and Yellow), again because of their jerseys; and the "Pentacampeões" (Five-Time Champions) because, well, they have won the World Cup five times!

Chile, "La Roja." Very simple. This nickname honors the team's famous red uniforms.

China, "Team Dragon." The name is a nod to the spirited style of play of the Chinese men's national team. The women's national team, on the other hand, is nicknamed "the Forceful Roses."

Chapter 4

Colombia, "Los Cafeteros." This South American squad gets its name from the large amount of coffee grown in the country. A *cafetero* is somebody who drinks or makes coffee. The women's national team in Colombia, though, has a very cool name: "the Powerpuff Girls."

Costa Rica, "Los Ticos." Costa Rican natives are called *Costarricenses*; "Ticos" is a shortened version of the traditional name.

Croatia, "Vatreni." The nickname means "the Blazers" in Croatian and pays homage to the passion of the players on the field and the fans in the stands.

England, "The Three Lions." The name refers to the country's rich history, going back to Richard the Lionheart, a king of England in the Middle Ages. The three lions that appear on the national team's crest also appear on the Royal Arms of England.

France, "Les Bleus." The boys in "bleu" got their nickname because of the blue color of their elegant uniforms. Classic and simple.

Germany, "Die Mannschaft." The nickname simply means "the Team." Leave it to the Germans to find a simple and practical name for their super-successful squad.

Ghana, "The Black Stars." The name refers to the black star on Ghana's national flag.

Italy, "Azzurri." The name means "the Blues." Unlike France, blue doesn't appear in Italy's national flag colors.

Chapter 4

Ivory Coast, "Les Elephants." The national team is named Les Elephants as homage to the ivory trade in the 19th century. "Ivory" is the name of the country, after all.

Japan, "Samurai Blue." Japan is another team that uses "blue" in their nickname. The men's team wore blue at the 1936 Olympics, their first major international competition. They beat Sweden 3–2, and they have worn blue for luck ever since! The Japanese women's national team nickname "Yamato Nadeshiko" is somehow less fierce and could mean either "a delicate pink flower" or "a woman with good traits that are rare."

Mexico, "El Tri." The name invokes national pride. "El Tri" is short for "El Tricolor" and refers to the three colors—red, white, and green—of the Mexican flag.

Netherlands, "Oranje." Named for the team's famous orange jerseys, the color refers to the old Dutch royal family, the House of Orange-Nassau. Since the team's biggest contribution to soccer is Total Football, the precise method of passing to keep ball control, the Dutch team is also nicknamed after the famous book and film *A Clockwork Orange*.

Russia, "Sbornaya." Another simple, but strong, nickname. *Sbornaya* means "national team" in Russian.

What's in a Name?

South Korea, "Taegeuk Warriors." The *taegeuk* is the symbol on South Korea's national flag. It represents a spiritual balance, like China's yin and yang symbol. The South Koreans are also known as "the Reds" because of the team's red uniforms.

Spain, "La Furia Roja." This nickname has two origins. "La Roja" comes from the red color of the team's uniforms, while "La Furia" describes the direct, aggressive, and spirited style of play in the 1920s, when Spanish players were a "fury" on the field. Lately, Spain is more often called "La Roja."

Uruguay, "La Celeste." Uruguay's "La Celeste" nickname refers to the team's sky-blue uniforms.

USA, "The Yanks." This name has been used to describe the USA's men's and women's national teams. Other names used by American fans include "the Stars and Stripes," or simply, "Team USA."

Other interesting national team nicknames include: "Princes of Persia" (Iran); "the Thousand-Mile Horse" (North Korea); "the Street Dogs" (Philippines men's team); "the Feisty Ladies" (Philippines women's team); "the Squirrels" (Benin); "the Crocodiles" (Lesotho); "the Boys Boys" (South Africa men's team); "Girls Girls" (South Africa women's team); "the Reggae Boyz" (Jamaica men's team); "the Reggae Girlz" (Jamaica women's team); and "the Most Serene" (San Marino).

Chapter 4

And What About Those Traveling Fans?

Fans all over travel the world to see their national teams play on the big stages. Some of these traveling fans have, of course, their own nicknames. Here are some famous groups of supporters from around the globe.

The Tartan Army is made up of the passionate traveling fans of Scotland's national football team.

Soccer may not be as big as football or baseball in the USA, but the so-called American Outlaws that follow America's national team are some of the loudest and fervent supporters around.

South Korea's supporters call themselves the Red Devils, and they are a colorful bunch.

Another "army" is formed by the Northern Ireland traveling fans, who call themselves the Green and White Army.

The Rojigans follow Denmark's national team all over the world, and they are famous for their red and white costumes.

Canadian fans like to keep it simple. The Voyageurs support Canadian soccer much like many other Canadians support ice hockey.

CHAPTER **5**

Luck and Other Crazy
Superstitions

To win, you have to be **good,** but sometimes you have to be **lucky** as well. Some players insist on having the same meal before each game, coaches might wear the same tie, and **superstitious** fans never go to the stadium without that lucky flag. **Luck** is important in all sports, and in soccer it can involve an octopus, **dirty underwear,** and a vanilla shake. Do you believe in luck? What's your **superstition?**

Chapter 5

An octopus named Paul was given the task of predicting match winners during the World Cup in South Africa in 2010. The octopus had to choose between two bowls, each with the flag of a team playing in a match. Paul picked the winner seven out of seven times.

Paul the octopus is not the only animal that has predicted the winners of World Cup matches. There is also Nelly the elephant, Flopsy the kangaroo, Shaheen the camel, Madame Shiva the guinea pig, and Big Head the sea turtle. That is wild!

Mexican player **Oscar Mascorro** has a few good luck habits before a game. He doesn't make his bed and always gets up on the right side of the bed. He also has a vanilla milk shake, a hamburger, and apple juice.

Luck and Other Crazy Superstitions

During the World Cup 1998 played in France, **Laurent Blanc** kissed the bald head of French goalkeeper **Fabien Barthez** before every game. The superstition may have had something to do with their success since France won the tournament that year!

• •

Real Madrid defender **Álvaro Arbeloa** likes to play with a coin in his right sock for good luck. It is said that Brazilian player **Robson** wore the same underwear while playing for an entire year. After a year of games, and smelly undies, he changed into a fresh pair.

• • • • • • • • • • • • • • • • • • •

The Colombian goalie René Higuita always wore blue underwear during his games.

Italian midfielder **Gennaro Gattuso** wore the same sweater every day during the World Cup in Germany in 2006. He also read Russian literature before every match. Maybe he did something right. Italy won the World Cup that year.

British legend **Bobby Moore** refused to come out of the locker room unless he was the last player to pull on his shorts before running out onto the field.

Kolo Touré (Ivory Coast) insisted on being the last player to get to the field and once got a yellow card for being so late on the pitch. Other players who like to be the last one on the pitch are **Lionel Messi** and **Cristiano Ronaldo**.

· ·

Sierra Leone player Malvin Kamara watched the film *Willy Wonka & the Chocolate Factory* before every game he played.

· · · · · · · · · · · · · · · · · · · ·

Some players, particularly strikers, don't like shooting on goal during the game warm-up. British striker **Gary Lineker** even said that he didn't like to "waste his goals."

Dutch legend **Johan Cruyff** punched his goalie at Ajax (**Gert Bals**) for luck before every game. He also liked to throw his chewing gum to the opponents' side of the field before games started.

Ukrainian coach **Valeriy Lobanovskyi** didn't allow any player to use number 13 on his shirt. He also didn't allow women to travel with the team during training and believed that a red-haired player was key for the success of his teams.

For Spanish coach **Luis Aragonés**, the problem was a color. He didn't allow any player to wear yellow during the team's trips.

Mario Gómez (Germany) doesn't sing the German national anthem before games. Gómez has been doing that since playing for the German U-15 national team, when he didn't sing the anthem and scored a goal.

Before each game, England's **John Terry** listens to the same music in the car, parks in the same spot, sits on the same seat on the team bus, ties tape around his socks three times, and cuts the tubular grips for his shin pads exactly the same length.

Many players think it is good luck to make their first step on the field with a specific foot: **David Silva** (Spain) always steps first with his left foot, while his teammate **Santi Cazorla** likes to do it with the right foot.

Other players don't like to step on the field lines until the game starts.

Argentinian goalie **Sergio Goycochea** was a specialist in stopping penalties. He thought it was good luck to pee in the middle of the field before a penalty kick series. He would do it surrounded by his teammates (since, of course peeing on the field is against the rules, and gross). This strange ritual worked so well for **Goycochea** that he did it during the World Cup Italy 1990 and during two decisive games at the Copa América 1993.

When Bayern Munich players Toni Kroos and Franck Ribéry had to decide who should free kick they chose by playing a playground game: Rock, Paper, Scissors. Weird? Not so much. Earlier in the same season, Borussia Mönchengladbach's players Marco Reus and Mike Hanke did the same thing.

CHAPTER 6

What in the
WORLD IS...?

**D**on't let your **teammates** (bad) or your coach (worse!) catch you off guard. You'll know all of soccer's **wacky** terms after exploring this easy guide to some common soccer **expressions.**

What is a **derby**? A **derby** is a **match** between two rival club **teams** from the same city or region. Most **derbies** have been played for years, and for the fans of these **clubs**, winning a **derby** is sometimes more important than winning the **championship**. **Derbies** are all about local pride—about whose **club** rules the city. Some famous **derbies** are Manchester City vs. Manchester United in England, Real Madrid vs. Atlético de Madrid in Spain, and Boca Juniors vs. River Plate, the two powerful **teams** from the city of Buenos Aires, in Argentina.

So what is a **clásico**? *Clásico* is a Spanish word that means "**classic**," and sometimes it's used in Spanish-speaking countries instead of "**derby**." However, **clásicos** can involve two rival **teams** from two big cities in the same country or even two different countries. In Mexico, the Super-Clásico between Club América and Guadalajara is the most important **game** of the year. The Spanish **Clásico** between Real Madrid and Barcelona faces two of the most powerful **teams** in the world against each other. In the national team **arena**, when the USA faces Mexico, when Brazil plays Argentina, or when England meets Scotland, people on both sides of the border get excited for an old **clásico**.

117

Brazil's biggest club rivalry—the clásico between **Flamengo** and **Fluminense**—splits the city of Rio de Janeiro in two. Known as

Fla-Flu,

this game has been played since 1912, when a group of unhappy players from Fluminense decided to leave the team and start their own club. They called it Flamengo, and since then two teams that used to be one have built one of the fiercest rivalries in soccer.

What in the World Is...?

CABJ

In Argentina, fans divide the city of Buenos Aires when their two top teams, Boca Juniors and **River Plate**, play each other in the annual Superclásico. Both teams started in the same working-class neighborhood in the city, but when **River Plate** moved to a more wealthy area, they started called themselves Los Millonarios, "the Millionaires."

BUENOS AIRES

Chapter 6

What is an **Olympic goal**? This is when a player scores a goal directly from a corner. The name "Olympic" was first used after the Uruguayan national team played a game against Argentina to celebrate their victory in the Olympics in 1924. The Argentinians scored a goal in such a fashion, and to mock the Olympic champs, they called it an **Olympic goal**.

What is a **Vuelta Olimpica**? You've probably seen teams doing a lap around the stadium after winning a trophy. Players and coaches parade around the stadium showing off the cup, flags, and sometimes even their little children. This is a "lap of honor," but it is known as **Vuelta Olimpica**, or "Olympic lap" because it was first performed after the Uruguayan national team won the gold medal for soccer in the 1924 Olympics.

Soccer -vs- Football

Soccer or **football**? The original name of the sport, association football, was created in England to distinguish it from other sports like rugby or football. In both sports, players could use their feet to kick a ball, so that makes sense. Many people think "soccer" is an American word that was created to differentiate it from American football, but in reality it is an abbreviation of the word "association" and was first used in England in the 1880s. Either way, **soccer** or **football** can just be called the beautiful game!

• •

What is a **treble**? **Treble** refers to something that has three parts, but in football's slang a **treble** is the incredible achievement that happens when a team wins three trophies in the same season. Only 23 clubs around the world have won a continental **treble** that includes at least one international competition. For example, Bayern Munich became the first German team to win the **treble** in 2013 after wining the Bundlesliga (German League), the UEFA Champions League (the top European club tournament), and the DFB-Pokal (German Cup).

Another achievement based on threes is the **hat trick**. In soccer, a **hat trick** happens when a player scores three goals in the same game. A **perfect hat trick** is when a player scores a goal with each foot and one with his/her head in a single game. To this day, **Pelé** remains the youngest player to score a **hat trick** in a World Cup. The Brazilian magician was 17 when he scored three goals against France in the 1958 World Cup semifinal. He also holds the record for most **hat tricks** scored in his career with 92!

The term "hat trick" comes from the game of cricket, and it is said that after a player took three wickets in a single game, the fans in the stadium collected some money in a hat and offered it to the cricket star!

Sometimes different traditions clash after a soccer game. In many countries when a player scores a **hat trick** he or she keeps the match ball as proof of the achievement. This is what British player **Geoff Hurst** thought after scoring three goals against Germany in the final match of the World Cup 1966, which England won. However, German striker **Helmut Haller** took the ball and walked with it to the locker room. **Haller** later said that in Germany there is an old tradition that, "If the winners get the cup, the losers get the ball."

HALLER

When a player scores two goals in a soccer game it's called a brace. "Brace," in Old English, means a pair of something (bird or animal) killed in hunting. "Brace" has its origin in Old French, though. So basically, when a player scores two goals, it is related to the act of hunting, hence scoring a brace.

What is a clean sheet? This is when the team's defense and goalkeeper don't allow any goals during a game or a series of games. Italian goalkeeper **Dino Zoff** holds the record for the longest stretch without allowing a goal in international matches. **Zoff** kept his clean sheet for 1,142 minutes, or almost 13 games. When it comes to teams, Brazilian club Vasco de Gama kept a clean sheet for 1,816 minutes, or more than 20 consecutive games!

What is **Total Football**? **Total Football** is a tactic in which any player can take the role of any other player on the team. It was made famous by the Dutch club Ajax and the Dutch national team in the 1960s and 1970s. By switching positions on the field, players could surprise the opposing team in ways not seen before.

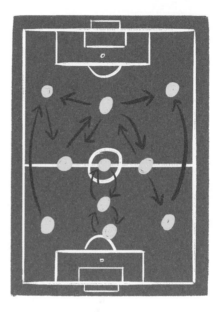

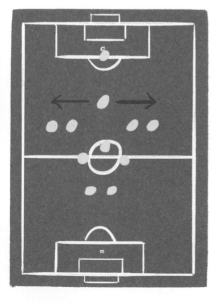

What is **Catenaccio**? It is a system based on a very strong defense. It was made famous in Italy in the 1950s (*Catenaccio* means "door-bolt") when coaches started using the position of the libero, or free defender (also called sweeper), who was positioned behind a line of three defenders to recover loose balls.

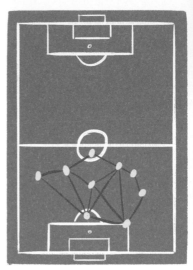

What is **Tiki-taka**? This funny name refers to the constant passing of the ball in a system based on keeping ball possession with short passes and lots of movement from all the players. It was introduced in Spain in the 1990s and became famous with the success of FC Barcelona and the Spanish national team. In women's soccer, the Japanese women's national team used a form of **Tiki-taka** to win the 2011 Women's World Cup by defeating stronger teams like Germany and the United States.

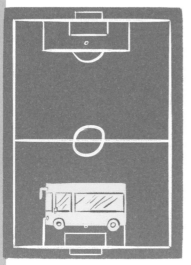

Can you "**Park the Bus**" on a soccer field? Well, not really, but when fans or commentators use this term it means that a team is using a very defensive strategy that puts all players in two defensive lines to avoid the opposing team scoring. Many people don't like this strategy because the team that **Parks the Bus** in front of the goal to avoid allowing goals is not interested in attacking. Some teams **Park the Bus** after leading with one goal and spend the rest of the game trying to keep that advantage. Not fun, but it works…sometimes.

What is a professional foul? This is when a player commits a foul on purpose to stop a dangerous play or when the team is caught off guard by the opponents. Sometimes it is committed to stop a player on a scoring position, but sometimes it's done only to stop the play when the team in defense feels a disadvantage. Not cool but you gotta do what you gotta do.

CHAPTER **7**

Soccer 101

You have your fancy tricks and can **dribble** an entire block of **defenders. Good!** But it will come in **handy** to know what is what and who is who in **soccer.** We will not bore you with the **rules** of the **game,** but here are some important **facts** you may want to know before lifting the **trophy!**

Professional soccer matches need four officials. The referee, two assistant referees, and the fourth referee. The assistant referees were not introduced in soccer until 1891. The fourth referee is a very recent addition and didn't appear in a major tournament until the 1998 World Cup.

The assistant referees move alongside the sidelines and help the referee with different tasks such as out of play, restarts, and offside. The assistant referees use flags to signal infractions to the main referee. They also communicate using small radios.

T he assistant referees used to be called "linesman" but in 1996 the term was changed to include women. Women referees and assistant referees can officiate games between men or woman.

The fourth referee is responsible for keeping records, checking equipment, substitutions, and displaying information. (They are the ones who show those electronic displays with time information and the players' numbers when there is a substitution.) If the main referee is injured and can't continue in the game, he or she can be replaced by the fourth official.

. . . .

Two more officials have been added in some tournaments. These extra assistants work behind the goal line and are there to help the referee with plays inside the penalty area. They are also in charge of making sure the ball completely crosses the line to avoid "ghost goals."

GOAL!

NO GOAL

NO GOAL

NO GOAL

NO GOAL

A ghost goal is when the referee calls a goal but nobody is really sure that the ball completely crossed the goal line. The rules of the game state that a ball has to cross the line in "its entirety." This means that if a teeny-weeny piece of the ball has not crossed the line it shouldn't be called a goal.

Ghost goals are annoying. Nobody wants to lose a game for a goal that never crossed the line. But don't worry; help is on its way! Goal-line technology has been used in some leagues, like the Premier League in England, to support officials. This technology uses electronic devices such as cameras and sensors to capture the exact moment the ball crosses the line. Many people think that goal-line technology will be used in all professional soccer games in a few years. Maybe one day you will see it in your league!

The rules of soccer state that players must wear "a jersey or shirt with sleeves." That seems to be a rule followed by everybody, or should we say, almost everybody, since in 2002 Cameroon's national team won the Africa Cup of Nations wearing a uniform with sleeveless shirts. When the team tried to use the same uniform in the World Cup later that year, FIFA banned the skimpy shirts.

Scoring a goal in a free kick is very difficult. And before 1927 it was actually illegal to score this way.

If your coach tells you that you will be "playing in the hole," don't go to the nearest pit! Playing in the hole is when a forward plays as a second striker and uses the space (or hole) between the midfielders and the attackers. Lionel Messi often plays "in the hole," so it's a good thing!

As opposed to American football or basketball, the soccer field doesn't always have the same dimensions. For international matches, for example, a field should have a maximum size of 82 x 120 yds (75 x 110 m) and a minimum of 70 x 109 yds (64 x 100 m). FC Barcelona's field at Camp Nou stadium in Spain has one of the largest fields in the world: 78 x 115 yds (72 x 105 m).

PROFESSIONAL CLUBS

Professional clubs are teams that hire players to join their ranks and participate in their local, regional, and international club leagues. A club like FC Barcelona plays in the Spanish local league called La Liga. It also participates in international tournaments, such as the UEFA Champions League. Barcelona has players of many different nationalities, such as **Neymar** (Brazil), **Messi** (Argentina), and of course players from Spain, like **Andrés Iniesta**, **Gerard Piqué**, and **Jordi Alba**. Although these players "belong" to Barcelona, they can also represent their countries and play for their national teams.

NATIONAL TEAMS

National teams are all-star teams that represents a country in international tournaments, such as the World Cup, the Copa América, the Africa Cup of Nations, or the Olympic Games. National teams consist of the very best players born in the country or who have been nationalized by the country they represent, regardless of which professional club they play for.

SOCCER ASSOCIATIONS

FIFA (Fédération Internationale de Football Association) is the leading soccer association on the planet, with 209 countries in its ranks. FIFA's main job is to organize and promote major tournaments, such as the World Cup and the World Club Cup. FIFA divides its members into six regional confederations: Africa (CAF), Asia (AFC), Europe (UEFA), North and Central America and the Caribbean (CONCACAF), Oceania (OFC), and South America (CONMEBOL).

Although it seems that FIFA rules the (soccer) world, the organization doesn't make or control the rules of the game. That job is the responsibility of the IFAB, or International Football Association Board.

CONCACAF (Confederation of North, Central America and Caribbean Association Football) represents 41 countries, including Canada, USA, Costa Rica, Mexico, and Jamaica. The USA women's national team is the most successful team of this region, with three  wins at the Women's World Cup. On the men's side, Mexico has won the U-17 World Cup twice and the Confederations Cup in 1999.

. . . .

CONMEBOL (South American Football Confederation), with only 10 countries represented, includes some of the most successful national teams in soccer history, such as Brazil (five World Cup titles, four Confederations Cups, five U-20 World Cups, and three U-17 World Cup trophies), Uruguay (two World Cup titles), and Argentina (two World Cup titles, six U-20 World Cup trophies, and four Confederations Cups).

OFC (Oceania Football Confederation) represents 14 countries and is perhaps the least influential of the world's confederations, especially since Australia moved to the AFC in 2006. In many of the OFC countries, such as Tonga, Fiji, and American Samoa, soccer is not the most popular sport. New Zealand is the only country in the region that has participated in a World Cup.

. . . .

UEFA (Union of European Football Associations) has 54 members in this super-competitive confederation. Although small countries like Andorra and San Marino belong to the UEFA, many soccer powerhouses compete here, such as England and Spain (one World Cup title each), France (one World Cup title and two Confederations Cups), Germany (four World Cups and two Women's World Cup titles), and Italy (four World Cup titles).

COMPETITIONS—NATIONAL TEAM TOURNAMENTS

FIFA World Cup

Played since 1930 (with some pauses during World War II), this is the largest and most important soccer competition on the planet. The World Cup finals are played every four years, but the tournament is actually really long: 209 nations compete for months to qualify for one of the 32 spots available in the final rounds. These final rounds played in a specific country are what we normally call the World Cup.

FIFA Women's World Cup

Played since 1991, this is the most important women's soccer competition. As in the men's tournament, countries all over the planet compete for months to qualify for one of the 16 spots available in the final rounds.

FIFA Confederations Cup

Since 2005, the Confederations Cup is played one year before the World Cup in the country that will host the tournament. It is played by the winners of each of the six confederation championships: UEFA's EURO, CONMEBOL's Copa América, CONCACAF's Gold Cup, etc., plus the host country and the FIFA World Cup holder.

. . . .

UEFA EURO Championship

Played every four years since 1960, this tournament faces off 24 European teams in a final round, usually played in one host country (sometimes two countries share the duty). Germany and Spain have each won the UEFA EURO Championship three times and are the countries with the most wins.

141

Copa América

This is the oldest soccer tournament played between national teams in the world. Played since 1916, the **Copa América** features 12 South American teams that belong to CONMEBOL, although in recent years they have invited teams from Central and North America to compete. To celebrate the 100th anniversary, the tournament was played in the United States and included countries from the entire American hemisphere. Uruguay has won this tournament 15 times, followed by Argentina with 14 wins, and Brazil, who has lifted the trophy eight times.

Gold Cup

Played every two years since 1990, the 12 countries that belong to CONCACAF face off to win the **Gold Cup**. Since it's played every two years, the winners of the last two tournaments play each other in a play-off to decide the team that represents CONCACAF in the Confederations Cup. Mexico and the USA are the dominant teams here, with seven **Gold Cup** trophies for the Mexican team and four for Team USA.

Africa Cup of Nations

Played since 1957, the **Africa Cup of Nations** is played every two years. Egypt has won the cup seven times; Ghana and Cameroon follow with four trophies each, and Nigeria with three cups.

Asian Cup

This is the second oldest continental tournament in the world. Played since 1956, it has been dominated by Japan, winners on four occasions, followed by Saudi Arabia and Iran with three cups each, and South Korea with two wins.

Olympic Games—
Until 1984 professional soccer players were not allowed at the **Olympics**. Since then, soccer's popularity at the games has increased, and today the men's national teams are formed by players under 23 years old, with three over-23 players per team. Since 1984, Argentina has won two gold medals on the men's side. Women started competing in the **Olympic Games** in 1996 with the USA's women's soccer team as the dominating squad with four gold medals.

Just like national teams compete against each other in international tournaments, clubs have their own competitions. Here are some of the most important!

COMPETITIONS— CLUB TEAM TOURNAMENTS

FIFA World Club Cup
UEFA Champions League
UEFA Women's Champions League
UEFA Europa League
Copa Libertadores
CAF Champions League
AFC Champions League
CONCACAF Champions League

A SUPER-FAST SOCCER ABC

Assist:
When a player passes the ball to another player who then scores.

Association Football:
Call it soccer or football, association football is the official name of the game.

Box:
Officially known as the penalty area. This is where the goalkeeper can handle the ball and where any fouls committed become penalty kicks.

Box-to-Box:
This is a term used to describe a midfielder who covers the whole length of the center of the field.

Cap:
A player earns a cap every time he or she plays for their national team. In the old days, players would actually get a little cap, or hat, to mark the occasion.

Counterattack:
It is also called fast break or a breakaway. It starts when the ball is taken by a team on a turnover from the other team.

Draw:
Simple. This is when teams are tied at the end of the game.

Nutmeg:
You nutmeg an opponent when you put the ball through his
or her legs.

Pitch:
A British term that means "the field." It's not just for soccer. It can be
used for rugby, cricket, and field hockey.

Playmaker:
A midfielder responsible for setting up attacking plays for the forwards.

Rabona:
A fancy trick where a player kicks the ball by wrapping around the back
of the standing leg. It's like kicking the ball with your legs crossed.

Rainbow Kick:
This is another fancy trick that happens when a player rolls the ball on
the back of one leg with the other foot to flick the ball over the head.

Volley:
When a player kicks the ball before it hits the ground.

Wall:
Defenders form a wall between themselves and the goal to try to
block a free kick from the opposing team.

Glossary

altitude:

The height of something counted from sea level up.

boots:

Shoes usually made of leather that reach above the ankle.

cleats:

Shoes that have wedge-shaped blocks on the sole to prevent slipping.

conceal:

To hide from sight. Also, to keep something secret.

dislocate:

To put a bone out of its normal position.

endurance:

The ability or strength to keep doing something hard for a long time, despite the circumstances.

goldsmith:

Someone who works with and creates objects made of gold.

handkerchief:

A small piece of cloth, usually square, for cleaning your face or for decoration.

nod:

A slight movement of the head downward to express understanding, agreement, or approval.

plaque:

A thin and flat piece usually of metal with words written to commemorate or as a reminder of something.

quarterfinal:

One of the four competitions whose winners will go to the semifinal game.

scantily clad:

Not properly clothed or underclothed for an occasion.

sheik:

A chief or leader in an Arab society.

suave:

Behaving smoothly and relaxed, in an elegant way.

United Nations:

International organization formed by most countries in the world with the purpose of promoting peace, cooperation, and progress. It is based in New York City.

valve:

A device for controlling the flow of air, liquid, gases, or other elements.

Resources

BOOKS:

Crisfield, Deborah W. *The Everything Kids' Soccer Book*. Avon, MA: Adams Media, 2015.

duopress labs. *Messi, Superstar*. Baltimore, MD: duopress books, 2016.

Hoena, Blake. *Everything Soccer: Score Tons of Photos, Facts, and Fun*. New York, NY: National Geographic Children's Books, 2014.

Jökulsson, Illuigi. *Stars of World Soccer*. New York, NY: Abbeville Press, 2015.

MATCH. *Incredible Stats and Facts*. New York, NY: Pan Macmillan, 2016.

Nagelhout, Ryan. *20 Fun Facts About Soccer*. New York, NY: Gareth Stevens, 2016.

National Geographic Kids. *Weird but True: 300 Wacky*

Facts About Awesome Athletics. New York, NY: National Geographic Children's Books, 2016.

Peterson, Megan Cooley. *Wacky Soccer Trivia: Fun Facts for Every Fan*. North Mankato, MN: Capstone Press, 2016.

WEBSITES:

www.factmonster.com/ipka/A0920619.html

mocomi.com/football-fun-facts/

outrageousfacts.com/sports.php

www.sikids.com/soccer

www.softschools.com/facts/sports/soccer_facts/576/

www.sportsforschools.org/interesting-facts/

Index

Here are some other books for curious minds from duopress:

9781938093579

9781938093326

9781938093531

9781938093777